Farfetched Farm:

Riding, Girlhood and a Lifelong Love Affair with Horses

**By
Aimee Wells**

Farfetched Farm: Riding, Girlhood and a Lifelong Love Affair with Horses

Copyright ©2023 by Aimee Wells

All rights reserved. No part of this publication may be reproduced, stored in a retrieval system, or transmitted, in any form or by any means without the prior written permission of the publisher, nor be otherwise circulated in any form of binding or cover other than that in which it is published and without a similar condition being imposed on the subsequent purchaser.

First Printing, 2023

ISBN : 9798376601150

Cover design by: Nathan Wells

Book Interior and E-book Design by Amit Dey | amitdey2528@gmail.com

This book is dedicated to Lowrey Jones – who will always be "Mrs. Jones" to me. You taught me how to be a horsewoman in every sense of the word and still inspire me to this day. Thank you for everything you did to create the wonderful oasis that was "Farfetched Farm."

FORWARD

My lifelong love of horses and the lessons they have taught me all began for me in one magical place during the late 1970s in a bucolic Northern California town that shaped both the equestran and the woman I would later become. Farfetched Farm was, of course, a real place – the home of my first horseback riding trainer and mentor, Lowrey Jones, and where I learned to ride and spent the majority of my waking hours from the age of 8 to 15. But Farfetched Farm was so much more than simply a physical location. It was a moment in time – for all of us "Fillies" lucky enough to pass through girlhood into our teen years on horseback under the guidance of Mrs. Jones. It was the late '70s and early '80s, a turbulent time in the world to be coming of age, but this magical place provided all of us horse-crazy kids with a safe and happy oasis from that chaos. It was my anchor then and continues to be today.

vi Farfetched Farm

So let's relive the past and visit the present. Hope y
"ride"!

Illustration of Farfetched Farm

INTRODUCTION

An adrenaline rush, mixed with pride in achieving a physical goal, a Zen sense of absolute presence in the moment, topped by the surge of loving joy from a favorite furry pet. Imagine if as a surfer, your favorite board was also a sweet, soft and loyal animal with whom you shared a special bond? Or consider if, as a skier, your skis were something that only performed for you and that called out your name with a nicker or blew warm breath into your face before you hit the slopes? This is the closest way I can describe the daily experience of riding horses for me and the reasons behind its driving obsession in my life.

It's the sport, the achievement of goals and competition, but it's also the physical experience itself -- the flying sensation of jumping fences and galloping down the line, and the total immersion in the moment, in your head focused and counting, breathing, without digital or emotional distractions. On top of all that, there's a living being working with you as a team, an animal with whom you've built trust and created a shared language. For all of these reasons and more, riding quite literally becomes much more than a hobby or a sport for those who fall hard and fast like me. For horse girls (and guys) like me, horses are closer to a lifelong addiction.

Probably the most important thing about horses that I've come to realize over the past 45+ years are the lessons they have taught me -- some of the most important lessons in life:

Lesson 1: Change is scary – but it opens up new worlds

Lesson 2: Persistence, discipline and hard work are the key to success

Lesson 3: Find your own joy as a way to tune out the other negative noise around you

Lesson 4: You can survive loss and go on to love again

Lesson 5: You <u>can</u> make your dreams come true – eventually – just not always on the schedule you had imagined

This book is a fond look backward to a moment in time of coming of age, not so long ago, but long enough to gain perspective. It's my way of sharing those life lessons as I learned them, about the horses and the bond you build with your equestrian partner – along with your equestrian tribe.

TABLE OF CONTENTS

Introduction................................vii

PART I..................................1

Chapter 1: Move-in Day.......................3

Chapter 2: Finding Farfetched Farm...........9

Chapter 3: First Lesson.....................15

Chapter 4: Settling into the Summer of '76..19

Chapter 5: Learning to Jump.................27

Chapter 6: Ponies on the Mountain...........31

Chapter 7: Sweet Surprise Arrives...........33

Chapter 8: The Horse Show Life..............39

Chapter 9: My Beloved (and Crazy) Quest.....47

Chapter 10: The Barn Family.................53

Chapter 11: Quest on the Rise...............59

Chapter 12: Headed South:
        The Annual Turkey Show............67

Chapter 13: The Crack That Changed it All 73

PART II 77
Chapter 14: After Quest - The Shuffle 79
Chapter 15: Velvet 83
Chapter 16: Teen Angst. 87
Chapter 17: Toughening up at Foxfield 89
Chapter 18: Junior High and Barn Boys 97
Chapter 19: The Maxi Taxi 101

PART III ONCE A HORSE GIRL 107
Chapter 20: Rediscovery 109
Chapter 21: Boundary Gate 111
Chapter 22: And Then Came Luc 115

PART I

MOVE-IN DAY

(Diablo, California / June 1976)

From the back of my parents' car, rounding the corner down our new driveway under the bright, mid-afternoon June sun, our new house gleamed white and fresh with promise of a new start in a new neighborhood. The two-story colonial-style home was surrounded by just over an acre of trees and greenery in the small town of Danville's affluent Diablo Country Club neighborhood. It was definitely a step-up from our last house in a suburban neighborhood about 25 minutes away.

"What do you think?" my dad said, as he turned the key in the lock and swung open the heavy forest green front door.

Bright white walls and gleaming oak hardwood floors shone in the summer sunlight streaming through the abundant floor-to-ceiling windows that framed a view across a verdant valley dotted with horses, a few houses and a golf course in the distance.

"It looks big. Where is my room?" I asked, as my five-year-old brother Zak and I dashed through the entryway, skidding across the wood floors in our socks "like ice skaters." We were eager to explore the two-story house that seemed much bigger and fancier than our previous split-level house in Moraga.

Truthfully, I was not actually an *easy* sell even at eight. I'd cried upon learning we would be moving away from my elementary school friends and pals on the Ashbrook Place cul-de-sac, from my Bluebird troop and the big grassy hill in our backyard where we slid on cardboard sleds and planted an "M&M tree." "Why do we have to go??" I'd wailed and cried. No child ever wants to move away from her childhood friends, school and familiar faces and places, and I was no exception.

Of course, back then there's no way I could have known that the move was not simply a "Movin' on Up" scenario, proof that my dad's corporate job had raised us to the ranks of country club dwellers. What it was, in fact, was a second chance for my parents' marriage. Picking up the pieces in the aftermath of infidelity, they had decided to "start fresh" in a new home, symbolizing a recommitment of sorts. And the house — filled with sunshine, shiny surfaces and surrounded by hills, trees, and horses — represented that hope and happiness were on the horizon again.

Moraga faded to a distant memory by the time I had climbed the stairs and dashed into the small bedroom at the end of the hall that I immediately claimed as my own. Never mind that there were at least three other bedrooms twice the size on the same floor. This one featured its own small balcony with French doors that, when propped open, allowed the scent of honeysuckle blooming in vines down the side of the house to waft in. But the piece de resistance? A broad window peering directly out across the backyard to a rustic red-and-white, two-stall barn below. A window from one of the stalls opened right up in direct view of the bedroom — the home of my future pony.

Much has been written about the almost innate obsession girls have with horses. And it's true, there does just seem to be a certain fever that illogically infects some people — most often female — from an early age, drawing them to equestrian pursuits, sometimes seemingly out of nowhere. For me, certainly ours was an animal-loving household full of pets of all kinds. My dad loves to tell the story of how he brought the family's two German Shepherds to visit my mom at the hospital window in the maternity ward after I was born. Later, a menagerie of dogs, cats, pet rats (yes, rats — Polly and Herman), iguanas and goldfish filled our home. But, horses were the pet I yearned for most, perhaps sparked by the first visit at age three to a farm where my grandfather "Poppie" set me on the back of a fuzzy pinto pony.

First pony ride with my grandfather, Poppie

According to my mom, I did hail from a line of equestrians on her side of the family. Her dad (my Poppie) and her brother (my Uncle Dave) had supposedly owned a cow pony they kept on some land in the Central Valley near Stockton, and I'd seen photos of him mounted on the horse in a cowboy hat. Perhaps that planted the seed? Later, I learned also that my mom's mother, my "Nonie," had also ridden English as a teen growing up in Stockton. Supposedly, she trained alongside famed hunt-seat champion of that era, Barbara Worth. However, her parents (my great grandparents) eventually forced her to quit due to fears she would get hurt jumping. As you might imagine, both my Nonie and Poppie were enthusiastic supporters of my riding and even helped where possible with some of the bills once I started showing.

But despite these roots, no one actively nudged me toward horses, and there were no obvious prompts pushing me in that direction at any early age. And yet, the obsession seemed to well up out of nowhere from my earliest childhood years. Living deep in the suburbs, not a farm in sight, I read horse books, drew sketches of a pony named Pride, and even mapped out architectural plans for a "barn" we could construct in the backyard. Suffice to say, the little red barn on the back of that Diablo house was quite literally at least a step toward this little girl's dreams come true.

"Mom! Dad! Did you see this? There's a barn in the backyard! I can get a pony, right?" I shouted down the hallway, begging my mom to join me at the window of my new room.

"Yes, it's pretty cool. We'll have to see about the pony. Maybe," she smiled, ruffling my stringy blond hair.

Suddenly moving to this new place, despite the prospect of facing third grade in a school without any friends seemed a lot less daunting. Because Diablo meant a chance to – possibly, maybe – have a pony of my very own. The trade-off seemed more than worth it.

View of our barn from the backyard

FINDING FARFETCHED FARM

One Saturday afternoon within a week of moving into the new house, we decided to take a family walk around our new neighborhood. Unlike Moraga, there were no sidewalks in Danville, and the houses were set farther apart, in many cases surrounded by acres of lush landscaping and sometimes even small horse barns just like ours. Set at the foot of Mount Diablo, the new neighborhood had steep hills, long driveways and few kids riding Schwinns or kicking balls around on the street. You were less likely to hear the tinkling of an ice cream truck than to see someone riding a horse down to the local post office.

Less than a quarter mile down the road and up and over what locals ominously called "Suicide Hill," we stumbled upon the end of a long Oleander-lined driveway leading up to an adorable white traditional home — and a riding arena that jutted out toward the street. The sign for the property read, "Farfetched Farm."

"Let's go check it out!" my mom said to my dad, brother and me, squeezing my shoulders as we walked up the drive.

Finding a miniature equestrian paradise filled with horses and young kids amid a residential neighborhood might have seemed a bit of miracle to us that summer day, but in truth it probably should not have been all that surprising, given the area's storied equestrian tradition. According to lore I later learned from local historians, Diablo actually began life as "the Railroad Ranch," a 10,000-acre plot for raising cattle and thoroughbreds, owned by "the Big Four" — Charles Crocker, Mark Hopkins, Collis Huntington and Leland Stanford. By the early 1900s, they had built a racetrack as a testing ground for the horses bred and raised there. Later, even after the track was long gone and replaced by golf course fairways, Diablo's horse culture lived on. Our street in particular, Caballo Ranchero Road, was specifically developed with plots of three to 10 acres each designed to serve as "ranchettes" for residents who wanted to live on miniature equestrian estates near the trails of Mount Diablo.

The Jones family — Lowrey, her husband Steve and their three daughters — had found their five-acre property at the end of Caballo Ranchero in the early 1970s. Though they later purchased adjacent land to expand to a larger 10-acre plot, the plan was never to operate a full-fledged equestrian operation. In fact, Lowrey says she originally started giving lessons on her daughters' horses as a favor to just three young girls whose parents had approached her. "I never intended to get any bigger than that!" she laughs. "It was always just something for fun, but our group just continued to grow."

It's not a stretch, however, to describe the setting of the Jones' farm as magical. It was quite honestly a bit out of a postcard fantasy plucked from stories set in the New England countryside rather than a California "ranchette." From the street, a long oleander-lined driveway curved up a gentle hill to a circle driveway fronting a charming white, Cape Cod-style, two-story home with black shutters, a brick-front walkway and verdant English-style greenery. From the iron "Farfetched Farm" sign at the bottom drive to the front porch and throughout the property, English hunt-themed motifs prevailed (think foxes, jumping horses, etc.). At the right front of the property at the top of the drive was a medium-size, sand-filled arena surrounded by a white fence and filled with hand-painted fences — not just poles and standards, but real solid fences such as a white "coop," a green turf-covered roundtop and a red-and-white "brick wall" (built from wood).

On that summer day, the arena was filled with about half a dozen horses and riders — all young girls wearing black velvet helmets, tan breeches and black leather boots. In the middle of the arena, giving firm commands, was a slim but sturdy woman with a silver blond bob and oversize sunglasses.

"Pick up the canter," the woman commanded as the girls and their mounts sped around her.

"Patty, don't forget outside rein, inside bend," she shouted to one long-limbed girl on a chestnut horse.

"Good, Gretchen. Eyes up, heels down!" to another.

We leaned up against the white fence around the arena observing the instruction until the lesson wound down, the horses were permitted to walk, and the woman strode over to our place at the fence. She was smiling — but in a tight and controlled way, signaling she was not quite sure of our intentions or in how much she should invest in this encounter.

"Hi! We didn't mean to interrupt your teaching, but we are new to the neighborhood and my daughter is crazy about horses! I'm Donna Grove, this is my husband, Dick, my son, Zak and my daughter, Aimee. She's a horse fanatic!" my mom blurted out.

Keeping my eyes averted, I had the urge to hide behind my mom. These girls were all real riders and they all looked older than me by at least a year or two. Why would they want me to join them? God, my mom was always so embarrassing.

The instructor strolled our direction.

"Hello. I'm Lowrey Jones. This is my home, and these are my students; my daughters also ride," responded the woman I came to know as "Mrs. Jones."

While it was difficult to see the steely blue eyes behind her glasses, the determined set of Mrs. Jones' pursed lips, her impeccable posture and the slight crows' feet spreading toward her temples illustrated a life spent in pursuit of disciplined outdoor activities. Mature yet ageless, firm and intimidating, yet oddly compelling, she reminded me immediately of the best teachers I'd had in my short lifetime to date.

One by one, the young riders began to steer their mounts over to the fence to check out the visitors. Mostly they were all smiling and patting their horses. How much fun must they be having? Did they all have their own horses? How in the world could I fit in when they all looked like they had been doing this for years and I had never even sat in an English saddle before?

My mom continued: "Would it be possible for my daughter to take lessons here, too? She's absolutely horse-crazy! She's been begging us for a pony for years and we finally even have a barn where she might be able to keep one."

Mrs. Jones gazed down at my eight-year-old freckled face and I finally looked up to meet her gaze.

"Has she ever ridden? I don't have many school horses, and I am not taking any new students right now. This is our family property and we keep a very small group," she responded.

"She's taken a few lessons in Western, but she is a beginner," mom conceded. "But you will never meet a more hardworking, diligent student, I promise."

Mom! Oh my god. This was humiliating, I thought. Obviously, this was not a fit. These girls had been riding for a long time, I was too little and too inexperienced to join this group.

"Sorry, but I just can't accept any more students at this time. You can stay and watch the rest of the lesson if you like, though," said Mrs. Jones, and then turned back to the surrounding riders. "Go on now - get back to the rail. How about each of you trot down over the X over there? And remember, heels down, eyes up!"

As we turned to walk home that afternoon, my mom reassured me. "Don't worry, Aimee. We will get her to change her mind. She just can't say no. We live right down the street, and I won't give up." And despite Mrs. Jones' discouraging words, I knew my mom was right. No one ever got in the way of my mom when she had her mind set on it or if her children's livelihoods were at stake. So while I was self-conscious and nervous about joining such an experienced group of equestrians, I had a very strong good feeling that my dreams were going to come true.

FIRST LESSON

It only took two weeks of persistent calls from my mother, begging and pleading and working every sales angle ("she can help muck stalls," "we live right down the street, so she'll be walking and we won't clutter your driveway with a car," etc.) to wear Mrs. Jones down. I was in — officially a member of the Farfetched Farm "Fillies" as we called ourselves. Lesson learned: Persistence works!

Lessons were to be twice a week, typically in the cooler morning hours before the blazing East Bay sun hit full force. Mrs. Jones instructed us to get outfitted at the local western wear store, Flanagan's, with the necessary equestrian apparel — paddock boots with a heel (so your foot wouldn't slip through the stirrup), stretchy breeches, leather chaps that zipped up the back of your legs, and most importantly, a black velvet-covered helmet (we called them "hard hats") to protect my noggin (despite the fact the helmet lacked any real chinstrap other than a simple band of elastic we pushed above the brim). And so, on that first day at "the barn," I was dutifully dressed in my new duds, stringy, dirty blond strands pulled back into a ponytail and ready for action.

"Good. You're just on time," said Mrs. Jones, stepping out of her back door and leading the way up the driveway past her home to the barn at the top of the hill where the horses were stabled. "We'll get your horse in just a minute; I think you'll be riding Happy today. But we have quite a few things to go over first."

And by a "few things," she meant the myriad details involved in safely handling, being around and caring for horses before your leg swung over any saddle. Mrs. Jones — a lifelong horse-woman raised in Maryland who had ridden in fox hunts and competed successfully as a junior on the East Coast — was a firm disciplinarian who believed in a program of complete horsemanship for her young progeny. Hers was not the kind of stable where riders were handed a fully groomed mount ready for a ride and skipped over all the messy stuff. Nope.

From day one we were taught — and regularly tested on — everything from how to groom your horse, and muck a stall, to how to soap and condition a bridle or name all the parts of a horse's anatomy. On days when stormy weather made riding impossible, we gathered in the Jones' house and got lessons and quizzes on horse anatomy and other principles related to caring for a horse, riding technique and tack.

That first day, against the backdrop of hot, dusty straw-filled air, I learned how to get my mount – a gentle, older chestnut Quarter Horse named Happy from his paddock and safely fastened into crossties to be groomed. I learned the proper technique for picking out dirt and rocks from hooves, how to curry comb, brush and towel away dirt and grime from his coat, which fly spray to use and where to apply it, how to set the saddle on just the right spot on Happy's withers and how to reach up and get the bit into his mouth and bridle over his ears, and how to walk him down the path to the arena before climbing onto a mounting block.

First lesson on "Happy"

Attracted to rules and structure, and an ever-eager-to-please "teacher's pet," I loved every minute of this strictly disciplined approach to horsemanship. And once I was able to feel the sway of Happy's walk under the saddle as I learned the correct commands for moving forward, stopping and turning, the rapture was complete. I couldn't wait to learn more, do more, go faster, get better and catch up to all the other girls I had seen in the arena that day. It was obvious from day one that the key to reaching that goal was putting in the work – practicing everything I had learned under Mrs. Jones' instruction, following every instruction to the letter, and even asking for extra lessons and exercises I could do at home when not in the saddle to continue my progress. If I wanted my own pony, I needed to be able to show I could do everything needed for her care and to ride confidently.

SETTLING INTO THE SUMMER OF '76

While my first few lessons were likely private sessions, within a few weeks I was settled into the regular routine of thrice-weekly group lessons with the rest of the Farfetched Farm crew. On lesson days (our schedule was mapped out in chalk on a large blackboard next to the barn tack room), you were expected to show up a half-hour early to groom and tack up your horse by the appointed hour.

Most of the other students already owned their own horses, but as a beginner, I was assigned one of Mrs. Jones' older schooling horses, usually Happy, Joe, Nick or Willy. I loved them all, but Willy, a flea-bitten grey schoolmaster (and former champion hunter) who had taught more than his fair share of tiny girls how to jump, had a special place in my heart with his tolerant, forgiving nature, seemingly undisturbed by the annoying mouth pulls and frustrated kicks of a beginner rider.

On the first day I walked into the barn to get ready to join my first group lesson on a Saturday morning, my heart pounded with nerves. I knew I was younger and less experienced than all of the other "Fillies." And my natural inclination as a slightly bookish and introverted eight-year-old was to keep my head down, try to blend in and not ask too many questions. Certainly, none of these other riders wanted anything to do with me. Turns out I was wrong.

"Hi! You're the new girl, right? Aimee?" said a tiny towheaded, freckle-faced girl with braids, stepping out of the tack room with a broad smile. "I'm Gretchen. Are you riding Willy?"

Willy taking me over my first crossrail, age 8

"Oh, I love Willy! He's so fun!" said another taller and slightly older-looking girl with brown hair and soft, kind eyes who was putting sugar cubes into a tack box in the aisle. "I'm Patty. Are you riding with us at 9?"

"Hey, did you bring a lunch?" asked another girl of about 10, popping her head out from around the corner. "Think we're going to go have a picnic on the hill after we give the horses baths. You could come if your mom doesn't care."

And just like that, I had been invited to the group. Joining a barn, I've come to learn is never just about the horses or riding. It's also about the "barn family" you're joining — the other riders with whom you're likely to spend more hours of your life than with your own relatives, other friends or classmates. At Farfetched Farm, this crew in the earliest days were a handful of equally horse-obsessed girls from Diablo just a couple of years older than me: Gretchen, Patty, Jennifer, Molly – and later, Annie, Elizabeth, Danny, Mandy.

Standing just a skootch over five feet tall and likely weighing less than 100 pounds soaking wet at age 11, Gretchen or "Gretch" as we called her, rode with a fearless, determined attitude and ferociously competitive streak. Her pony Peanut (and later, a gorgeous mare named "See the Light") was a bratty but talented little Bay, and the two of them were an unbeatable combination. Off her pony, Gretch was a sweet and smart girl, ever helpful and responsible.

On the other end of the stature spectrum was Patty — a tall, coltish, brunette tween with impossibly long legs and a soft-spoken and measured demeanor. Equally talented as Gretch,

22   Farfetched Farm

Gretch & "Lizzie" or "See the Light"

Patty was a quiet and elegant but strong rider well-suited to her big thoroughbred hunter. Outside the arena, Patty was a brainy bookworm who came from an irresistibly nerdy family of readers and writers. As someone who had been teased for years about being a dork who preferred books over people, Patty and her family seemed like kindred souls.

Molly was the oldest rider. Already a full-fledged teenager in high school by then, Molly towered over all of us at an imposing 5'11". With dark hair and glasses, Molly was the oldest in a big Catholic family with six kids and served a similar "big sister" role among our group. She rode a thoroughbred mare named "Out of Sight."

And then there was Jennifer. With sparkling blue eyes, bob-cut dark blond hair and a 100-watt smile, Jen cut a striking appearance even at the preadolescent age of 10. But it was her bigger-than-life, slightly offbeat and always entertaining personality that really made her stand out. Jen was the jokester of the group, always outspoken and opinionated. She was the first to suggest a trail ride on the mountain, or to break out a backgammon chest or spark up a Monopoly game between classes at a show. Jennifer rode a big, dark, somewhat mule-like Bay horse with a tendency to pin his ears back named Summer Wine.

Farfetched Farm Fillies, original crew. Patty Freeman on Bo, Jennifer, Molly, Kirsty, me, Ginger, Gretch on Peanut

There were other students who came to join our group shortly after my first year at Farfetched Farm (including Mandy Porter, who became a famed professional Grand Prix jumper and trainer), but Jen, Gretch, Patty, and Molly formed the core crew who showed me the ropes at the barn in those first few months. And we spent a lot of time together on those long summer days.

After lessons finished in the late morning, no one ever rushed to get home. Even after bathing our horses and polishing our tack — all the while a tiny transistor radio hanging from the wall blasted tunes from the local top 40 station -- we'd lounge around on tack boxes, snacking on pomegranates picked from bushes on the trail to the arena, chatting about our horses and riding (and later, about school and boys). Often, we'd set up obstacles around the yard that we could "jump" as if we had imaginary horses under us, competing in hunter and jumper courses on foot. Sometimes, if the Jones' were out for the day — inevitably instigated by Jennifer -- we would even hop the fence into their backyard, sneak into the bathhouse to grab a suit and take a dip in their pool.

The prospect of getting caught was terrifying of course. Mr. Jones, a stockbroker by weekday and gentleman farmer on the weekends, was a gruff and intimidating presence around the barn. Tall and lanky, with a demeanor that always seemed to us kids to be a bit irritated by the flanks of children underfoot on his property, Mr. Jones scared the bejeesus out of us when he drove his tractor around or reminded us of something we left out of our tack boxes. We knew that if we were in that pool and the Joneses showed up, we were dead. So, the minute we heard anything in the driveway, out of the pool and over the fence we went, even if it meant into the dirt without a towel or suit!

Equally intimidating and yet also awe-inspiring to all of us young riders at the time, was the Jones' teenage daughter, Brooke. While both other Jones girls had ridden and taught lessons, it was Brooke who had leaned into the sport most from a competitive standpoint at an early age. Blond like her mom and sisters but especially slim and long-limbed like her dad, Brooke fit the Hollywood casting part of a female equestrian: serious, strongly disciplined and athletic. To watch her ride, when she hopped on one of our horses to help school during the week, was to watch sheer talent in motion. Her position in the saddle was always flawless and even the naughtiest of horses straightened out under her aids. Because she'd been flagged from an early age as a future champion, Brooke actually trained with a legendary horsewoman in Los Angeles, Marcia Williams, who everyone called "Mousie." Just about every weekend, the 16-year-old would catch a flight and spend the weekend riding and going to A-rated horse shows with Mousie's barn.

LEARNING TO JUMP

Up, down, one-two, one-two, one-two. I focused on lifting out of the saddle in direct rhythm with Willy's outside leg as he trotted down the rail of the arena — posting on the correct "diagonal" as my instructor, Mrs. Jones had taught me earlier that summer. The sun shone brightly on that late August afternoon, turning the skin on my ears and nose pink and causing droplets of sweat to trickle down my neck. But I didn't feel the heat at all.

"That's right, Aimee, good. Keep your eyes up, heels down, elbows in," Mrs. Jones commanded from the middle of the ring. "Now walk, then pick up the canter."

Deepening my seat into the saddle, and a slight squeeze of the reins, Willy, a sweet-mannered flea-bitten grey gelding with the patience of a saint, complied with a change in gait. Walking was definitely his favorite speed. I sneaked a small pat to his withers and whispered, "Good boy," before shifting again into position to ask for the canter.

"Remember, bend him a little to the inside, hold your outside rein and kick with the outside leg," urged Mrs. Jones.

Following her directions, I squeezed, scratched, and then kicked Willy hard with the outside leg, and he propelled forward into the rocking chair motion of the canter. We floated around the ring again and again, my wispy blond ponytail flowing out under my helmet and flipping against my back with every stride. This was much more fun than the posting trot.

"OK, how would you like to do a little jumping today?" Mrs. Jones asked after we'd slowed again to a walk to take a small break.

I looked over at my mom, who was watching quietly from a bench under a tree next to the arena and smiled. She smiled back with a thumbs-up.

"Yes! For sure!"

We started with trotting crosspoles — poles placed to look like giant Xs that help riders and horses stay centered in the middle of a fence.

Peering out through and above Willy's speckled grey, pricked ears, I pointed him toward the first fence at the end of the arena. "Trot, trot, trot, trot" I hummed under my breath as we approached the middle of the X, catching it just as he lifted his knees to heave his body over the one-foot obstacle then cantered away.

"OK, now canter the two fences down the diagonal," shouted Mrs. Jones. "Keep your leg on, and your eyes up!"

"OK, Willy, let's go, buddy," I whispered, kicking the elderly schoolmaster as we rounded the corner and started across the middle of the ring toward the first of two 18-inch crosspoles set on a line. I poised up above the saddle, knees bent, hip angle slightly open in the two-point position and grabbed a tuft of his grey mane. "One-two-three, one-two-three, one-two-three, jump!" I counted silently as we seemingly flew over the tiny fences, gaining speed as we jumped down the line in six strides.

"That was so fun! Can we go again?" I asked, as I leaned down to hug my panting mount.

It's hard to overstate the overwhelming mix of joy and adrenaline washing over me with those very first jumps. Within those first 10 minutes what had begun as a general affinity toward horses as oversized pets shifted quickly to obsessive addiction. To feel like you're flying while in communion with a thousand-pound animal, knowing you helped make that happen all on your own at eight years old and 75 pounds without a lick of fear and realizing this was a special gift you had all to yourself. No matter what else might be happening at home or in the world I knew I had this incredible thing — horses, jumping and a magical world called Farfetched Farm — that was rare and sacred.

PONIES ON THE MOUNTAIN

Not all my saddle time that summer of '76 was spent in riding lessons. Unlike its current manicured McMansion existence, in those days this wealthy suburban neighborhood was still decidedly "horse country," with horses outnumbering golf carts (or at least it seemed). More homes than not featured a small barn or equestrian facilities in a back or side yard. And people were happy to let young horse-crazed kids help and even ride unaccompanied or guided by adults. I learned this — much to my overwhelming joy — the first time one of the "Storm twins" who lived across the street showed up at my front door around the time I'd started up at Farfetched Farm.

"Hey, you're new here. I'm Tania, and this is my sister, Kate," said the young girl of about 10. She had big, deep-set eyes, stringy, long, dirty blonde hair and wore a T-shirt and dust-smudged jeans; her taller, teenage sister stood behind her looking bored.

"We live up there," she said, pointing to the house perched on a hill across the street. "Kate has a horse, but we sometimes help out a lady named Mrs. McMasters — you know that barn three houses down with all the ponies? If you help her muck out the stalls, she'll let you ride 'em up the mountain. Wanna come?"

"Um, wow. Mom? Can I go ride with these girls?" I yelled over my shoulder. "I'll go get my helmet. That sounds cool."

Before long, bombing around the neighborhood and even up the trails of Mount Diablo bareback on one of the McMasters' Shetland ponies was almost a daily occurrence. Kate, Tania and I would meet at the neighbor's property, muck a stall or two and then throw bridles on the bratty little ponies for a day of trail-riding. I don't remember ever meeting or even seeing an adult connected with these ponies — Mrs. McMasters supposedly approved of our adventures and/or I never heard otherwise.

Under the consistently hot, dry July sun we'd sweat in our jeans as we steered the little devils through trails, sometimes racing each other across open fields, eventually finding a shady spot to dismount and eat snacks we'd brought along. It was often almost dusk by the time we meandered home, and by that time, the ornery ponies were eager to get back to the barn for dinner. Once my pony cut out in a dead gallop home, impervious to the bit and my frantic cries, breaking into a trot only to dip his head down and charge toward the wooden siding of the barn. I heard the denim of my pant leg rip as the pesky bugger scraped me against the barn hoping to dismount the annoyance on his back. It wasn't until later when I got home and jumped in the shower that I saw the bloody gash from the nail that had pierced my knee. Never felt it that day, and the next day I was back on the pony, back on the mountain trails.

SWEET SURPRISE ARRIVES

By the end of that summer, with about two and a half months of lessons under my belt, I was not only running through all three gaits (walk, trot, canter) easily, but trotting over crosspoles and learning to jump. It was about time to find a pony of my own.

Around the same time as I started third grade in the new school, Mrs. Jones had convinced my parents it was time for me to graduate from her school horses to a pony of my own. I'm not exactly sure where she was found or how she was chosen, but seemingly overnight a 14.2 hand, bay Morgan "pony" with a fuzzy white star on her forehead named Sweet Surprise, ("Cindy" for short) arrived to take residence in the little red barn behind the house.

Equipped with books on horse care and maintenance and surely the guidance of Mrs. Jones, we set about the challenging — and to this 8-year-old — exhilarating task of keeping a horse in our backyard. That meant twice-daily treks down the path, sometimes in the dark of morning before school or in the pouring rain into a pitch-black barn to feed, water and let Cindy out, muck her stall, clean tack and check on the mare's well-being. Sometimes mom helped, but more often than not, it was a solo task that required overcoming natural childhood fears of spiders, snakes and boogeymen in the shadows.

Mom and me on Cindy in the pasture

One morning, I slipped on my rubber rain boots in the garage on an early dark winter morning headed out to toss Cindy her morning breakfast alfalfa flake. Sliding my toes down into the right boot, I suddenly felt something hard and wiggling in the heel of the boot. As I screamed and pulled my foot out quickly, I peered down to see a squirming potato bug that had found a dry home in my shoe.

In the hot dry Indian summer, in addition to the tarantulas that wandered off the mountain to breed and were often found scurrying around our property, snakes were another constant threat. One late Sunday afternoon, I pulled the rolling barn doors apart calling out Cindy's name when I was suddenly stopped in my tracks by an unmistakable ratting on the cool dirt floor inside.

"Dad!!!! Mom!!! Oh my god!! There's a rattle snake in the barn!!" I screamed as I tore up the hill to the house seeking help. Truth be told, I was less terrified about getting bit myself than about Cindy falling prey to the deadly venom. My poor dad, a man with a life-long phobia of snakes, swallowed his fears, picking up a heavy shovel and trudged down to the barn to "take care" of the problem by beheading the rattler.

When it came to the riding itself, at least five times a week, I hopped on Cindy and rode up and over "suicide hill" a quarter mile down the road to Farfetched Farm for lessons. And that little "ride" was not always uneventful, given the never-great combination of flighty horses and absent-minded motorists sharing a road. At least once if not a few times, a spooked Cindy, alarmed by a wind-blown branch or unexpected car exhaust tossed me and clattered down the street into some startled neighbor's backyard.

Overall though, Cindy was a great first horse — tolerant, sturdy, cute enough and only slightly naughty but never

Hanging with first pony, Cindy, summer of 1977

mean-spirited the way some true ponies can be. Sure, she would charge back to the barn around dinner time, but her ears were rarely pinned, she almost never nipped (unless she mistook your fingers for carrots) and she was always game for bareback double rides around the pasture when I'd hop on her with my mom or a friend for fun. Even most of my school friends — horse-oriented or not — got to join in the fun. After school, I'd pop a pink fuzzy bareback pad on and ride down to a neighborhood friend's house for a visit, invite them to join me on her back and ride over to the Diablo post office to pick up our mail. And because Cindy lived within ear and eyeshot of my bedroom, I was able to wish her a "sweet dreams, sweet girl!" from the window every night.

THE HORSE SHOW LIFE

Despite feeling like a house pet, Cindy was up to the task of teaching a little girl to ride. First of all, she could honestly jump the moon. She may not have been the fanciest pony in terms of conformation or form, but with more "go" than "whoa" as they say in the horse world, Cindy could bomb around 3-foot courses with ease.

So by winter of that first year with Cindy it was time for my first horse show. Equipped with a used Stubben saddle, off-the-shelf boots and a hunt coat sewn by my aunt, we entered a small schooling show to test my skills and our rider-pony partnership. Unlike later "rated" shows where we trailored the horses and stayed for days near the venue, this first show was a local affair to which we all simply rode our self-braided mounts through the neighborhood (and back home again). Setting off in the damp, foggy dawn hours in shiny boots, our hair tucked into hairnets under our helmets, with parkas over our hunt coats, the Farfetched Farm team headed to Kimberwicke arena about two miles across town.

Once we arrived, we met up with Mrs. Jones and all the parents and family members eager to shine our boots, serve up donuts and wish us good luck before we warmed up before the first classes.

As the youngest member of the barn crew, I watched some of the older, more experienced girls ride in the bigger fence classes first, cheering them on from the back of my pony and trying not to get nervous. When it was finally our time to enter the ring for the first class - 2-foot crossrail hunters - my dad shouted, "Go dink!" from the stands as my teammates, brother and mom all looked on.

The rest honestly is a blur. I don't remember winning or even how my round turned out. It was about two minutes of flying

Kimberwicke schooling show. From left: Summer Wine & Jennifer; Molly Freeman & Out of Sight; Cindy & me.

around the ring hopping over tiny fences with my ponytail flipping on my shoulders and smiling on the way out as my friends and family hooted and hollered encouragement. As I left the ring, I leaned down and threw my arms around Cindy. "Good girl! Good girl! You're the best pony in the whole world!"

By the time summer of '77 rolled around, Cindy and I had started to hit our stride competing with the rest of the Farfetched Farm "Fillies" at numerous "schooling shows" (unrated local shows where no braiding was required, fees were low and the emphasis was on practice and learning rather than prizes). That summer we also accompanied the rest of the girls to the annual Golden State horse show in Santa Rosa — a rated show where points counted in the regional horsemanship association annual awards and competition stepped up to the next level. Outfitted in my baggy, homemade hunt coat, off-the-shelf boots and secondhand saddle, riding a sweet but far-from-fancy-moving pony-sized horse, I was woefully unprepared for this new world. A world in which some of the horses in my classes sold for tens of thousands of dollars, the clothing was all custom-made and tailored, ordered from specific select European brands, and everyone sat in the bleachers when not riding critiquing the rides and horses of others throughout the day.

While we enjoyed the experience — chocolate milkshakes and Frito pie from the snack bar and polishing our boots in the motel room at night being some of the highlights — we brought home few ribbons, and it became clear that it was again time to move on and up the horse ranks again.

Getting Cindy ready at Golden State Show

The annual Santa Barbara Turkey Show" held over the week of Thanksgiving every year provided the perfect turning point to take that next step. An A-rated competition that featured several of the year-end medal finals for riders who had qualified at shows throughout the year, the Turkey Show was one of the few times Farfetched Farm ever made the journey to Southern California. All the best of the best — riders and horses — across the state came together in this one event every year. Suffice to say, Cindy was not really Santa Barbara-caliber.

Because I was not quite ready to officially "trade up" from Cindy (and I'm sure Mrs. Jones was still working on my parents to consider opening up the budget for a more show-quality mount), we found a short-term solution that fall. His name was The Mighty Wizard ("The Wiz" for short) and he was the semi-retired former champion hunter of a friend of Brooke's on loan or lease to us for the fall. When he arrived, Wiz, who'd been pulled out of pasture for this last hurrah, was round as a roly poly, his white coat matted with green manure stains and his tail muddy and full of burrs. Sweet-natured, calm and lazy, the rangy gelding slowly but surely regained some of his former luster after several baths using "blueing" to bleach out his coat, along with a rigorous grooming routine. And in the ring, Wiz was a bit of an automatic machine — or what we used to call "push-button": a schoolmaster who knew his job and once you cranked him up, kept him cantering and pointed him toward the fences, he would carry you around to ribbons.

Part of the fun in the annual Santa Barbara show was competing in the costumed jumper teams for the younger age divisions. Didn't matter if you or your horse usually only ever rode in the hunters (a competition judged on pace, form and style, similar to figure skating). At Santa Barbara, you also took them in the jumpers (where all that counted was speed and faults from knocking down a rail) so you could partner with two other riders in the same age group to compete as a team, bombing around 2'6" fences against the clock. Prizes were given out for best and most creative team costumes in addition to flawless rounds. That year, Mrs. Jones arranged for me to be on a team with "the Flood twins" — Lisa and Karin Flood, two talented young riders from San Francisco with whom we often competed at other shows. My mom sewed the costumes — we were the Pooh Bears, which involved red shirts and fuzzy yellow ears affixed to our helmets — and I remember dropping them off at a large Edwardian mansion in

Pacific Heights prior to the show. It wasn't until years later living in the San Francisco that I realized the Flood girls were a part of *that Flood family*, i.e., famous San Francisco descendants of 19th century silver baron James Clair Flood whose family name graced several landmark buildings in the city such as the Flood Mansion and the downtown Flood Building.

The Might Wizard or "The Wiz" at Santa Barbara Show 1977

That was definitely part of the riding experience then — and still is today, i.e., realizing that the scrappy kids you were hanging around with in the bleachers and at the back gate had names recognizable to most Americans. Like Folger. Or Firestone. Or Carlin. Or even Newman -- as in Paul Newman, whose daughter showed and who often wandered around the Santa Barbara fairgrounds.

MY BELOVED (AND CRAZY) QUEST

Wiz was an awesome horse but alas just a temporary solution. With an outgrown pony and ambitions to show in the 3-foot-fence, 11-and-under division at rated shows, I needed a horse with talent enough to compete but at a budget my nonfamous family could afford.

According to Mrs. Jones, one solution to this dilemma was to find a promising younger "green" horse to bring along. Similar to purchasing a fixer-upper and hoping your sweat equity will pay off when you trade up to another house down the line, the goal was to find a horse with potential and the right demeanor to put up with a still-learning rider while in training, who might eventually be worth several times her purchase price. With that goal in mind, we traveled down to Los Angeles to try a 7-year-old Quarter Horse mare at Mousie's barn who looked to fit the bill.

Pretty sure I fell in love with Quest the minute Mousie's assistant walked her out of the crossties. Standing 15.3 hands with a glossy blood bay coat, three white socks and a lightning bolt-shaped white stripe down her face, along with beautiful almond-shaped eyes, she was unquestionably striking. And her personality on the ground and under-saddle was sweet, calm and honest. While she'd never jumped more than a cross rail nor competed in a single show, she sailed calmly and easily over everything I put before her that first day. Mrs. Jones declared her form over fences — knees tight and together, neck arched — to be excellent, and her gaits, especially at the trot, to be lovely. "She's an amazing mover," Mrs. Jones exclaimed as she watched us trot around the arena. For $2,500 —a bargain price for a horse of her quality even in 1978 — this was a Santa Barbara-worthy mount in the making.

"Quest" aka "Sing Softly"

It wasn't long after we got Quest home, though, that we started to learn at least one big reason why her price had been so reasonable. Possibly due to prior abuse or a horrible accident, Quest was insanely, irrationally head-shy. The mare would simply not allow anyone to touch her ears. No amount of coaxing, soft cajoling, carrots or any other treat worked. This was a major obstacle primarily when it came to getting her bridled, a task that required lifting the leather headpiece and browband up and over her ears. Such a job is never easy for children, but this took it to a whole new level. So there we were. The proud owners of a horse that effectively could not be ridden other than in a halter.

We tried sending her away for a couple of weeks to a "cowboy" who was said to be a horse whisperer/miracle worker for difficult cases like her. It didn't work. She came back exactly the same. I cried. My mom cried. Pretty sure Mrs. Jones cried, albeit behind closed doors.

That's when we decided to get creative. Why not simply lose the browband and fasten the bridle via the side straps, forgoing the necessary task of pulling her ears under? For shows, we created a browband that included Velcro on the underside that could be removed and added after the bridle was on without touching her ears.

The system wasn't perfect, of course, and we hadn't ever fixed the underlying issues. For example, before every show when we needed to trim the fuzz around her ears — or do any kind of grooming on the top half of her face really — we had to have our vet tranquilize her before we could get anywhere near them. One time, while getting her usual preshow trim, the drugs started to wear off and Quest suddenly woke up, jerking her head up and rearing out of the crossties until she bashed her forehead into a lightbulb on the barn ceiling. The resulting gash requiring several stitches certainly didn't help this issue.

Despite this one complication, Quest quite immediately became the love of my young life. From the minute I woke up until I went to bed at night, all I wanted to do was be on her or by her side.

More than ever before riding had become an oasis and escape from many of the more stressful things in my young life, and Quest was one of the best friends I had. At home, while the loud nighttime fights between my mom and dad had somewhat subsided since our move to Diablo, there was still often an undercurrent of strife and sadness between them. My dad traveled often, leaving my mom to manage Zak and me on her own, and she often seemed lonely and depressed or preoccupied with some new diet or exercise regime.

Meanwhile, at school, I struggled with bullying and taunts from other kids who teased me about being tall, wearing glasses, being a dorky "teacher's pet" (aka, straight-A student, so uncool) — as well as being obsessed with horses. While I longed to be one of the cute, petite, popular girls with tons of friends, I spent most of my school days feeling like an ugly outcast and oddball.

"What's wrong, you big oaf? Did you lose your glasses? Why don't you go try to find them on the playground?" shouted a girl named Ann as she shoved me out of the girl's bathroom onto the playground asphalt where a boy named Jamie was waiting to pummel me with his fists. This was just one of many instances that would be labeled "bullying" in today's more enlightened times.

Another time, on the last day of school on a hot June day, I found a folded triangle of paper with a note on my desk reading, "Better watch out. We've all got water balloons in our desks." I looked up and around. Most of the boys and a few of the girls were giggling and staring back at me with cruel, taunting faces as we all awaited the final bell. After appealing to the substitute teacher for sympathy, I was allowed to leave class 10 minutes early that day to avoid being pelted by two dozen 11-year-olds wielding water balloons. I hid in the kindergarten playground behind a slide until seeing my mom's Toyota Celica pull into the pick-up zone.

But at the barn, all of those troubles and insecurities dropped away. From atop Quest, peering through her ears down the path to the arena or headed toward a fence, I was invincible. No one else at my school had this — this skill, this bond with an animal and the life filled with accomplishments and older friends. I hugged my horse and buried my face in her warm coat, knowing that when I was with her, she made me feel that I was the luckiest girl in the world.

THE BARN FAMILY

Because Quest was a true show horse rather than a backyard pony, she lived at Farfetched Farm in her own stall in the barn at the top of the hill on the Joneses property, along with "Richard" and "Lizzie," "Bo," and "Summer Wine." So the minute I got home from my fourth grade classes and changed, I charged down the street to see her, bringing armfuls of treats such as sugar cubes, apples and crackers. As I walked up the drive and the barn aisle came into view, the mare would typically peek her head out of the stall, nickering, seeming to sense my presence even before I called out her name.

"Quest loves it best when I wear my yellow shirt. She always nickers when she sees me in yellow," I told my mom. "And she really loves Cheez-its. Can you buy me another box?"

At Farfetched Farm, we didn't have trainers or assistant trainers riding our horses several times a week or even full-time help turning out the horses as it is today at most of the barns where I have ridden as an adult. Owners were expected to be there at least five to tix days a week to ride and care for your horse — rain or shine, school functions or finals, family obligations or not. And I couldn't be more thrilled. There was absolutely nowhere in the world I'd rather be than breathing in the warm, sweet air of the barn in Quest's stall or peering through her ears from atop her back.

With Quest in my life, I now spent nearly every waking hour outside of school or sleeping at Farfetched Farm — or on the road at a horse show. Right after arriving home from school, after grabbing a handful of Mother's chocolate chip cookies and throwing on my riding clothes, I trotted down the road each afternoon. The transistor radio hanging from a nail on the side of the barn was almost always on, playing tunes from local top 40s station KFRC, while all of us riders laughed and talked and told jokes as we groomed our horses in the crossties.

"Aimee, do you know what this song is about," teased Jennifer, never missing an opportunity to rib me for being the youngest (i.e., most naive) member of the barn. "You know, 'Ladies of the Night'?"

I had to admit, I had no idea, something that cracked all the other (also older) girls up.

"It means 'hooker,' you know, a woman who has sex with a man for money, silly! I mean, what else don't you know?" Jen howled.

The thing about it is that Jen's teasing was good-natured and in no way as mean-spirited as the kids at school, who loved calling me names until I cried. She and the other barn girls

Jennifer jumping Summer Wine

treated me like a little sister needing education and guidance, who was also sometimes the source of a giggle or two. I loved it. With just a brother, I'd always longed for sisters, and now I had a bunch.

At the shows, our families traveled as a group, staying at whichever was the closest Travelodge or Best Western motel where we could run back and forth between each other's rooms to polish our boots or gossip about the other horses and riders we'd competed against or watched at the show. On the showgrounds we roamed in packs hitting up the snack bar for nachos or snow cones to consume while watching classes from the bleachers or the back gate as we cheered on our friends.

It's hard to recall any petty gossip or mean-girl antics between our tight-knit group. As an adult where I've seen this kind of behavior spiral out of control between riders at barns dominated by junior competitors, it's hard to believe. But at Farfetched Farm, we truly lived the motto of sportsmanship or as Mrs. Jones preferred to call it, "horsemanship." We were each other's biggest fans, congratulating each other on our victories and encouraging each other through falls and failures.

Holidays were a particularly special time for the Farfetched Farm "Fillies" (though by this time, we'd actually added one boy to the group, Danny, making the term a bit of a misnomer). Every year in the week leading up to Christmas, we'd pick one night to decorate the barn and our horses' stalls. With the radio blaring and our excited chatter filling the frosty nighttime air, we'd drape tinsel garlands and hang colored lights around each stall, hanging stockings we'd fill with apples, sugar cubes and other gifts for our horses to be presented of course on Christmas morning. It was a competition of sorts to see whose stall decor was the most elaborate and/or creative.

There was also the annual Farfetched Farm holiday party. Riders and their families crowded into the beautiful Jones home to celebrate the year's achievements and accomplishments while munching on cookies and sipping hot apple cider. The highlight of the night was the presentation by Mrs. Jones of special prizes for such honors as the "Super Pooper Scooper" (best tidying up after your horse), "Best Sportsmanship" and "Most Improved Rider." Usually, we also presented our beloved and sometimes feared instructor with a special gift we'd purchased or made ourselves, such as a homemade quilt with individual patches sewn by each of us depicting our horses or other riding imagery.

The quilt we sewed for Mrs. Jones for the holiday party

QUEST ON THE RISE

To Mrs. Jones' credit as a talent scout and with the help of frequent catch rides from her superstar equestrian daughter Brooke, Quest progressed fairly quickly within our first year together. In our lessons at Farfetched Farm, Quest picked up most of the basics with ease, including flying lead changes (Horses need to "lead" with their inside legs when cantering around an arena and when changing direction, to swap to the opposite legs. To successfully compete in most of the hunter-jumper divisions, this execution must be flawless.) Brave and willing, she had what trainers like to call "a great brain," meaning she could figure out where to take you and how to find her way out of any distance in front of a fence, from a solid half-round to the brick wall and the chicken coop in our arena. Within a few months, it was time for our first show.

It was a sunny morning in Bakersfield, California, as I studied the course of freshly painted and flower-adorned fences from the back gate. Not only was this technically an A-rated show, it was also our first time "off the property together" as they say, and I could feel the tightness through my chest signaling anxiety. With the exhale of a deep breath, the back gate swung open and I walked into the arena.

"Next on course, number 220, Sing Softly and Aimee Grove."

Circling at the canter past the judge's stand as Mrs. Jones had advised, I forced myself to take a deep breath. Heels down, eyes up, count, stay in rhythm, "One-two, one-two, one-two." Quest's black-tipped, long ears pricked expectantly as we headed to the first fence on the course: a 3-foot white gate on the diagonal headed away from the back gate. Propped up off her back, maintaining a steady canter step and eyeing the top of the fence then the ground in front of it, I tried to focus only on distance. "Where's my spot, god, where's the spot?" I panicked inside, then let out a breath of relief when I saw it, knowing my mare was headed just to the perfect "spot" for taking off in front of the fence.

No distance seen as a rider means making scary decisions to either push for a jump from farther away or to contract the stride to take off from deeper near the base. Making the wrong decision can result in a stop or worse a crash right through a fence.

But on this day, at our very first show in our very first class (Children's Hunters 11 & Under), Quest and I seemed perfectly in sync, with her seemingly finding all these distances in her own stride. We rounded the far side of the arena, ignoring the flapping paper bag outside the fence and the shuffling bystanders in the bleacher seats, headed down the five-stride line on the outside. Jumping into the line required clearing a set of white poles stacked above a brush box with fake pink flowers then cantering straight down the middle to a hefty looking roundtop topped with another white pole.

"One-two, one-two, one-two, jump." We were over fence one of the line, opening up in a robust canter down to the second fence, "one, two, three, there it is, four, five, go," I thought as we easily sailed through the line and began to round the corner again.

"Good girl, sweet girl," I whispered to Quest as we headed up through the middle of the arena on the diagonal toward what seemed to be a massive three-foot oxer (two fences propped next to each other spaced by a couple of feet creating a wider obstacle to clear). With a long approach such as this, there's an inordinate amount of time for a rider to gain anxiety and lose confidence in his or her sense of distance. "Should I lengthen my stride? Should I close my leg and just simply grab the mane, fix my gaze at some point over the jump and simply let fate take over?" These are the thoughts going through my head as I headed toward that evil oxer that day.

In the end, the final decision I made turned out to be the wrong one, as Quest lost confidence in her equally green rider and skidded to a halt, toppling me from her back straight into the center of the two fences. I held onto the reins as I crashed and tangled in the poles, afraid the mare would run off and somehow hurt herself.

Brooke and Mrs. Jones quickly ran over to pluck me from the wreckage and walk Quest away from the scene. "It's OK, you're OK, she's OK," said Mrs. Jones as we walked out of the arena and back to the barn. "Everybody falls. The important thing is to get back on and fix it. Plus, she's just a baby."

Falling off Quest in first 3-foot class at Bakersfield Horse Show

"She's just a baby." This was a refrain I heard a lot that year as Quest and I tried to guide each other at shows and at home while training. But it sometimes wasn't easy to keep a positive attitude when others in my classes and even in my barn were riding mature, been-there, done-that horses, what we called "push-button" hunters.

Annie, a new girl just one year my senior who'd started at Farfetched Farm around this time fit that description. Petite, brunette and spunky, Annie was a gutsy and disciplined rider, with an older teenage sister who also rode. Annie's mount was a mare named Jezebel. Jet black with white stockings and a stripe down her face, "Jezzie" was striking and well-trained. Unlike Quest, she'd been around the show circuit and knew her way around a hunter course, with auto-changes and nice rhythmic, predictable gait over fences. They were undeniably, a hard pair to beat.

While Annie and I didn't compete directly in most classes because of our age difference, the competition did exist from a psychological standpoint. I watched her classes and her wins with a twinge of envy. Even though I loved Quest with all my heart and knew she and I had a special bond, it was hard not to wonder how great it might be to soar around the course by simply pointing and kicking on a well-trained horse who already knew her job? Maybe then I'd have more blue ribbons and silver platters, or become high-point contender for the Northern California annual rider of the year in the 11-and-under division, rather than continually starting and stopping, crying, training and learning? Wouldn't it be fun to just have fun rather than work so darn hard?

But work hard we did, and Quest continued to progress. That summer at the Golden State summer horse show at the Santa Rosa state fairgrounds, Quest and I were champions for our respective divisions (hunter under saddle for her, hunt seat equitation for me). I had even managed to win and qualify for the Onondarka Medal, which meant we'd be eligible to compete in the Onondarka finals at the annual Santa Barbara Turkey Show that fall. The Turkey Show (named for the fact it typically ran through the week of Thanksgiving) was the biggest, A-rated show of the year and the only time nearly everyone in our barn traveled south to compete. It was a show we all looked forward to and trained for all year.

A page in "Horses" Magazine was a big deal

Note: "Medal" classes at horse shows are special classes judged on the rider's form and execution on the horse and around the course, otherwise known as "equitation." The talent and form of the horse's jump or gaits are not a factor, though a flawless round over a complex course of fences and challenging exercises, as well as riding in perfect form, are required for a win. Once a rider wins the specified medal class (back then in addition to the Onondarka for riders 11 and under, there was the ASPCA Maclay, NorCal, Barbara Worth, CPHA and a few more), they qualify to compete against all the other riders who have won that same medal class at other shows around the state in one big "medal final" class at the end of the year.

HEADED SOUTH: THE ANNUAL TURKEY SHOW

Nestled in blankets with my brother in the back seat of our Chrysler Cordoba on a darkened pre-dawn morning in November, it was hard to tune out the AM radio broadcasting from the front speakers. My parents had the news on as we headed down the 101 that day to Santa Barbara, towing two horses in a rented trailer behind us.

"Reports are coming in that the congressman has been shot, we are not sure yet if it is fatal," reported the news anchor who I could hear clearly in the dark. He was reporting about some horrific happening across the world in a place called Jonestown or Guyana, or Jonestown, Guyana? I wasn't sure. I knew this was probably not something we should be listening to as kids, so I stayed quiet, hoping my parents didn't shut the radio off.

"Yes, it's been confirmed, Congressman Leon Ryan is dead from a fatal gunshot wound. We are also learning more about what appears to be a mass suicide among the followers of Jim Jones, leader of the People's Temple in Jonestown. Hundreds of men, women and even children appear to have died from some sort of mass poisoning ...." the frightening news droned on in the darkness as we drove along southward, until my mom finally insisted my dad turn it off.

"I just can't listen to this anymore, Dick!" she said, snapping the dial to off, shifting us into silence for the next few hours.

Just a couple of hours later, we experienced a nightmare situation of our own. Pulling off the freeway to get gas, a small white car zipped in front of ours, cutting us off before the stoplight. "Shit!" my dad yelled, slamming the brakes in order to avoid hitting the motorist in front of us. Not that I knew anything about driving at all, let alone driving a car towing a horse trailer filled with two fancy show horses, but I had a pretty good feeling this was not going to end well. Burnt rubber smell filled the car and we heard the squeal of our car skidding on the asphalt as the trailer behind us fishtailed. Then we heard a thud.

"Oh my god, oh my god, oh my god! Dad! Oh my god! One of the horses is down!" I yelled.

"Dick, get over to that gas station now!" my mom demanded.

After pulling into a side area of the Texaco station, we all jumped out of the car and ran to open the window of the trailer to find out what had happened. Turns out I was right. Jen's horse whom we had agreed to haul to the show, had lost his footing and fallen in his cramped side of the trailer, smashed against the metal divider and unable to get back up. On the other side, Quest was frantic, spooked and scrambling to free herself from the confined space.

"We have to get him out," I commanded. The logic was that we would unload both horses, and then remove the middle metal divider. But before we could do anything, we had to calm Quest down.

"Sweet girl, it's OK, it's OK," I spoke to her, as my mom gripped the lead line, I'd clipped to her halter through the window opening. She was trying to hold down her head so that she didn't rear up and hit it on the top of the trailer. Unfortunately, Quest threw her head up as my mom's arm was propped against the metal window opening, scraping the flesh down clean eight-inch gash from wrist to elbow. Blood gushed everywhere, down the white trailer, across my mom's shirt.

Onlookers from across the way who happened to have a horse van as well, ran over to help. We grabbed a clean towel and wrapped it around my mom's arm.

"We'll take her to the ER. She's going to need stitches." I was crying. My mom was crying. My six-year-old brother was crying as my mom climbed into the stranger's car, headed to the ER.

Meanwhile, we still had to get the horses out. Somehow, once Quest was out of the trailer, we were able to remove the divider, enabling Richard to get his footing to stand up again. He seemed flustered but miraculously uninjured.

"How about we take the horses down to Earl Warren for you, and you all go help mom at the hospital? We have two extra spots and it's no problem," offered the good Samaritan also headed to show at Santa Barbara.

Soon we were in the hospital at my mom's side. She was bandaged up after getting 15 stitches down her arm, but ready to head back out. We hit the road again and managed to make it to the showgrounds by nightfall.

While that was the most dramatic incident of that year's Turkey Show, it was not the only excitement. For one thing, the fall of 1978 brought an abnormally abundant amount of rainfall to the California coast. From the start of the ride down 101, drizzle and a light rain through grey skies kept the windshield wipers whirring. And by the time we arrived that night, light rain had turned to torrential downpour. Given all the arenas were outdoors and uncovered, the footing turned quickly to slushy, gushy mud and puddles. We rode through it, wrapping our velvet helmets with plastic covers, washing out our breeches at night with Woolite, scraping the dried mud from our boots with butter knives.

Despite the rain and mud, this was also the year of the celebrity sightings at Santa Barbara. During our barn's annual restaurant Thanksgiving meal at a fancy place called El Encanto, we heard our parents whispering about a famous actress named Diahann Carroll who was dining nearby, encouraging us to follow her into the restroom to ask for an autograph. (She complied).

Later, my dad spotted Charles Bronson watching his wife compete in a flat class, caught Paul Newman wandering around the showgrounds (his daughter, Clea rode in the 15-17 division), and watched as my little brother ventured up to say "hi" to actor Leslie Nielson, who was popular that year from his star turn in the hit movie "Airplane."

Finally, one night we heard the show would be closing down early for a movie that was going to be filming in the main dome arena. Exhibitors were welcome to come watch from behind the ropes, and when we found out that it was Farrah Fawcett of "Charlie's Angels" fame who'd be playing an equestrian in the arena, just about the entire show crowded into the wings to catch a glimpse. Adding to the excitement was the fact that Farrah's boyfriend, Ryan O'Neal and his teenage daughter, Tatum, would also be in the stands watching the shoot.

"Wow, look, there they are," murmured the crowd, edging out to get a closer look at these bona fide "stars."

"Wait, Aimee, isn't that your brother?" gasped one of my barn mates.

And sure enough, there was six-year-old Zak, seated about 50 feet away in the "secured" area next to Ryan and Tatum, smiling and laughing. Somehow, he'd snuck his way past the security to "say hi" again. When Ryan saw the adorable strawberry blonde, freckle-faced boy with the infectious grin, he invited him to sit with them.

Of course, my mom and dad knew they had to reclaim their child, so they told the guards and were allowed to move behind the ropes to get him.

"Great kid. He's trading my autograph for candy bars. Let him stay a while. It's cool," joked Ryan, as my dad apologized for the interruption.

All in all, despite the dramatic start and less than auspicious weather conditions, we put in a good showing at Santa Barbara that year. Quest was champion in her under-saddle classes, I won an equitation class or two and placed well in our hunter courses. By the end of the show, Mrs. Jones had actually even received more than one inquiry from other trainers wondering if this "cute, flashy mare" was for sale. According to her, Quest's value had tripled since we had purchased her just about a year before. In the year ahead, with my 11th birthday still on the horizon, I had at least two years to build up a show record in the children's hunters and try for the coveted (12-and-under) Ononarka Medal.

Life outside of the barn for me was still abysmal. School bullying and loneliness plagued me as I struggled to overcome the labels my classmates had assigned — "four eyes," "teacher's pet," "weirdo," "big oaf," and, of course, "horse girl." But in the arena, on the show circuit, at the barn, things were on the upswing.

THE CRACK THAT CHANGED IT ALL

About three months after the Santa Barbara show on a bright February morning with blue skies dotted with the cloudy remnants of the past week's stormy weather, I decided to let Quest out to run off some of her frisky morning energy before going for a ride. The early morning air was brisk and the wet, sandy footing of the arena crunched under her hooves as we stepped in and I closed the gate before unlatching the lead line from Quest's halter, freeing her to gallop, buck and play. And then, amidst snorts and slapping hoofbeats, came an unmistakable loud crashing, cracking sound — the sound of a hoof meeting the wooden fence.

I looked up to the end of the arena and caught sight of something that froze my 11-year-old heart: Quest, slowly cantering down the side on three legs, the fourth dangling limply without touching the ground. Somehow in her exuberance at turnout after a few rainy days cooped up in the barn, the mare had kicked out and injured herself. It looked bad, but I had no idea how bad it was.

Since it was only about 8 a.m. on a Sunday morning, no other riders nor even Mrs. Jones was at the barn. And given we were still at least two decades away from the advent of a mobile phone, I literally had no way to call for help.

Somehow, I managed between panicked tears to run up to the stables and find one of the boys mucking stalls who could help me catch Quest so I could get to the barn telephone. However, even then, it was a conundrum. Mrs. Jones and her family were at church. And my parents were in Puerto Rico, traveling for my dad's job on a cruise ship for the company's sales execs while we stayed with my aunt. I wasn't sure if there even was a way to reach them, even if I had a phone number and wasn't worried about astronomical long-distance charges.

The only option was to phone the vet and wait for the Joneses to arrive back. After what seemed like hours at the time, both the vet and Mrs. Jones were there. Soon, I was shuffled away from my horse and into the house while the two met as he examined Quest. I was only 11, but I still knew this was a very bad sign.

Inside the house, I phoned my aunt.

"Auntie Carole, can you please come get me? Something bad happened to Quest. The vet is here and I'm waiting to talk to Mrs. Jones," I told her.

This was the second animal emergency in the span of five days during my parents' trip. Just earlier that week, Zak and I witnessed our dog, Tara, get hit by a car in front of our eyes. The neighbor where we had been staying had asked us to call Tara behind the station wagon to get her to come home. She didn't want the dog in her car and figured this was the best way to get her back. What she didn't figure was that the squirrely German Shepherd would veer out to the side of the tailgate just at the same moment as a car behind us decided to try to pass on the top of a hill.

"Oh my god, no, Tara no!!" I screamed at about the same time we heard the screech of brakes, thud of impact and the cries of our childhood pet slammed to the asphalt in front of our eyes.

With a broken back, hips and internal bleeding, Tara was in bad shape. Most families would have contemplated euthanizing her the first night. But we begged and pleaded and cried over the long-distance lines to the ship, and my parents agreed to have the dog transported to UC Davis animal hospital for emergency care. She was still there, recovering from surgery, when the Quest accident happened days later.

Now, sitting in the New England-influenced, fox hunting-themed family room of the Jones' family home, I sat patiently on the couch across from Brooke, trying hard to stop crying and be a brave girl. I nibbled on oatmeal butterscotch chip cookies and took a deep breath as Mrs. Jones entered the room and took my hand.

"Aimee, I need to tell you that Quest broke her leg. Unfortunately, honey, there is nothing anyone can do when a horse breaks their leg. They don't heal like people do and they can't wear casts. I'm so sorry honey."

I looked up, knowing the answer but asking it anyway. "Do we need to put her to sleep?"

She nodded and patted my hand again.

My next memory is only of looking out the window of my aunt's car seeing my sweet mare standing in the arena with the vet as we pulled away down the driveway, the last time I would ever see her.

PART II

AFTER QUEST – THE SHUFFLE

If you ask my mom today, she'd say "nothing was ever really the same again" after that day. And it's true in many ways. Quest's death meant the end of true, bonded horse ownership for me and was certainly my first true deep heartbreak and loss. Forty years later, I would continue to have the recurring dream that someone, somehow has "found" Quest, that she never had actually died, and I could have one last ride with her. Certainly, Quest's accident also precipitated some of the worst times for our family, including the unraveling of my parent's marriage.

But it really wasn't as simple as that. I didn't quit riding. I didn't fall off the ledge, rebel, run away from home, or find myself in the typical teenage troubles of many of my peers. I just kept getting back on the saddle as Mrs. Jones instructed me to do, doing whatever it took to keep horses and riding in my life. (*Lesson 4: You can survive loss and go on to love again*).

Within a month or so of Quest's death, after crying for days and nights on end in my room or in my mom's lap, I finally mustered up the courage to wander up the road to the barn again and see my friends, watch a lesson and chat with Mrs. Jones. She'd already been in touch with my parents, proposing solutions to my current situation -- i.e., lack of a suitable mount to continue my equestrian career. Evidently, there was a sweet and talented liver chestnut, 16-hand mare for sale at a decent price who she'd like us to consider.

"Aimee, I know she will never replace Quest, but this mare could be a good match for you, and we can try her at Indio," explained Mrs. Jones when we sat down in her parlor after the morning lesson. Her steely blue-grey eyes looked straight into mine, and the message was clear. Riders kept going. It was time to mount up again.

So, off we went to Indio — a big A-list horse show held every spring in the California desert - to try a new horse. I missed Quest every single day and I knew that no horse was ever going to replace her and the place she had in my heart. But I also knew that I loved riding far too much to give it up, even if that meant going on to ride without her.

The trainers walked the liver chestnut mare out with a saddle and helped me mount for a test drive. Surprisingly, I liked her. A lot. Less green than Quest with a decent show record, the chestnut mare was cute and fun, a good match for my riding quirks and ability. While I was definitely still mourning Quest, I started to dream about the ribbons I could possibly win with a more seasoned mount like this. Her price was $7,000, and my mom agreed she was "a good deal." My dad, however, had other opinions.

I could hear the fighting downstairs in the kitchen as I lay in bed.

"No. We are NOT buying another horse. Absolutely not. We cannot afford it, and this is not the time for this kind of commitment!"

"She needs a horse, Dick! This is Aimee's whole world. She's a good girl, her heart is broken. Can't we do this for her? I'll find a way to help pay for this, my parents can help," my mom reasoned.

The arguments seemed to continue for a few days, but as I would learn throughout my life again and again, timing is everything and it wasn't lining up in my favor this time. My parents told me we could not afford to buy the mare.

VELVET

To her credit, neither Mrs. Jones nor my mom gave up looking for solutions to finding me something, anything to ride, even just temporarily. That's about when Velvet arrived.

Owned by a friend of Mrs. Jones and "loaned" to us in exchange for care and board, the petite black mare took up residence in the backyard barn at our house in the stall next to my pony, Cindy, who was currently being leased to a little girl in the neighborhood. Not necessarily a fancy hunter needing the higher-end accommodations of Farfetched Farm, Velvet was deemed more of a temporary fill-in for lessons and my affection.

We never really bonded, though Velvet was sweet and simple enough. She generally would jump most of the fences you pointed her toward, got most of her lead changes and didn't have many nasty habits, other than the general bitchiness some mares demonstrate during their "heat." However, at just a little over 15 hands and fine-boned, she was not the right proportion for my growing tween frame, nor truly talented enough for the hunter ring, thus not a longer-term option.

For several months though, Velvet gave me a mount to ride in lessons and compete at a few shows. Until tragedy struck again.

It was a winter afternoon, and I was in the house doing my sixth-grade homework when I heard loud screaming from the barn and a pounding on the back door. It was the little girl from next door who leased my pony, Cindy, and she was hysterical.

"Oh my god!! Aimee!! Mrs. Grove! We have to call the vet!! Oh my god! Velvet got hurt! Her leg is bleeding, it's really really bad!" she gasped through a torrent of tears.

I'm honestly not sure if I simply blocked this memory out, if my mom physically blocked me from seeing the gruesome injury, but the images from this day are blurry. From what we learned through the girl ("Michelle") and the vet who was called for the urgent emergency visit, Velvet had been out grazing in the pasture surrounding the barn and smaller corrals. Somehow Cindy, who'd been tied up in her stall as Michelle was tacking her up, had broken away and out the corral gate, which had been accidentally left unlocked. The two mares, freed together in the larger pasture for the first time, tusseled, with Cindy ultimately kicking Velvet in the forehand. The kick had been so hard as to not just break the bone but nearly sever the lower part of Velvet's leg, leaving her hoof dangling from a tendon and blood gushing out everywhere.

I couldn't go down to the barn. I couldn't face it. It had been less than a year since seeing close to the same thing with Quest and I was not even officially a teenager yet. Like Quest, Velvet was "put to sleep." Because they administered the lethal drugs in her stall, getting her body out and to the horse crematorium was a problem nobody seemed to have anticipated. Even as I cranked up music and covered my ears, I could still hear the loud crashing from my bedroom as they knocked the stall walls down so they could get the trailer in to remove her. For years, even after the blood had been washed away, I was never able to go into that stall again for fear I could catch a glimpse of the horrific scene in the barn that night.

TEEN ANGST

Velvet's death was not the only tumultuous and trying event of my sixth-grade year. It was also the year my dad moved out of the house again for the second time after my mom had discovered the affair with his secretary. Between the demise of their marriage and his efforts at starting a new career as an entrepreneur in the entertainment industry, buying me a horse was not a huge priority for the family. Finances were a little shaky, my mom was an emotional wreck, and chasing equestrian accolades simply had to take a back seat.

All this turmoil coincided, of course, with my own "coming of age" — i.e., getting my period for the first time. It was the holiday break, in that week between Christmas and New Year's. I'd turned 12 just a couple weeks earlier and had no friends my own age who had gone through this yet or at least that I knew about. Most of all, I could not imagine anyone like Doug, the boy from school upon whom I'd developed a mad crush, ever give me the time of day if he knew this disgusting thing was happening to my body.

Not that Doug had shown me the slightest indication of interest even prior to this momentous event. In fact, on the last day of school before Christmas break following the sixth-grade holiday "dance," I had gifted him with a giant Hershey's chocolate kiss before running off to the school bus. Sitting down on the bus a few minutes later next to my friend, Sheri Perlow, she informed me that she and Doug were now officially "going steady." Not only was I crushed, I was humiliated too.

But now the period thing seemed to seal my fate forever.

"No one my age has their period," read my diary entries from that time. "I'm a total freak. It's so gross, and I feel so sick. I can't even go out because what if I bleed on my pants and everyone sees? I can't believe I'll be dealing with this horrible thing for the rest of my life!"

As always, I tried to bury my schoolhood stresses and emotional anxieties in riding and the relative haven of the barn and my Farfetched Farm friends. However, given the musical chairs nature of my horse situation and my adolescent, erratic hormone levels, this was not easily managed as in the past.

TOUGHENING UP AT FOXFIELD

Crying is something that has always come easily to me. Naturally sensitive and self-conscious, I've always battled tears as the first reaction to any hard situation, especially when disappointed in myself, and especially when it comes to riding. Too many times, after a poor round in the arena at a show or following a stupid mistake in a lesson at home, I'd spontaneously erupt into sobs of shame and self-loathing. "I suck, I should quit, there's no use. I wish I could disappear," ringing through my head in an endless loop.

Crying, of course, was 100 percent against the rules and decorum of the horse show world, however. We were expected to hold our heads high, suck it up, accept the critiques and simply suit back up and try again until we got it right. "There's no crying in baseball" is a famous line from the movie "A League of their Own," and at least on the tight ship run by Mrs. Jones, the same could be said of riding and horse showing.

Despite this unwritten rule, my emotions got the best of me more often than not. At one show, I forgot the course midway through, realizing it suddenly as I looked up and wasn't sure which was the next fence. There was a slight shuffling in the crowd of onlookers before the announcer proclaimed, "Rider is off-course." Suddenly a flush of heat spread up my face and neck and I could feel the familiar swell of tears rising up and then streaming down my cheeks before I could even exit the arena.

"That was terrible! What's wrong with me?" I sobbed to my mom, who ran up to me as I walked out the gate. I could see Mrs. Jones' disappointed face, despite the pat she gave my knee, telling me "It's OK. There's another class tomorrow. No need to cry."

Perhaps unsurprisingly, my parents got a call from Mrs. Jones soon after that fateful day late that spring of my sixth-grade year asking them to enroll me that summer in a sleep-away horse camp in Southern California called Foxfield. "Aimee needs to toughen up a bit," I was told she said, pointing out that the camp structure of riding many different horses and trying many different activities from vaulting and cross-country to dressage, trail rides with girls from all over the country, would be a valuable experience. On board with the plan, my parents booked a two-week stint at the exclusive camp and I set out for the adventure about a month later.

Located in the tony, semirural town of Sherman Forest in Southern California's San Fernando Valley, Foxfield was (and still is) a magical fairyland for horse crazy kids to live, eat and breathe English riding against a gorgeous outdoor backdrop. Situated on what seemed to be hundreds of acres of canyon land dotted with trees and rolling hills, the Foxfield summer camp operated out of a handful of low-slung, dorms-style buildings built around a swimming pool and adjacent to the Foxfield Riding Academy. These camp accommodations were situated across a small gulley from the main riding facilities, which consisted of several barns and pastures spread across the vast property, along with at least three outdoor arenas and a broad cross-country course dotted with natural fences like stone walls, logs and ditches.

Arriving the first night after being picked up, saddle in tow, from the Burbank airport, I warily eyed the slightly drab camper "barracks." On the positive side, I could see a side area shaded by large trees that contained a perfect set of miniature jumps just the right height for teenage legs to clear. "Jumping" on foot, pretending to canter like a horse and clear jumps as if you're riding an imaginary horse, is a favorite pastime of just about any equestrian of any age when given the chance. We spent hours at Farfetched Farm setting up courses with brooms and hay bales and lawn chairs, "competing" with each other in imaginary hunter or jumper rounds. Here, the jumps were built and painted to look just like the ones you'd see in the show ring - an 18-inch brush box, a 2-foot "brick wall," etc. This was a good sign.

"That looks pretty fun, right?" said a petite blond girl with a freckled nose and clear blue eyes who was following my lead into the camp housing.

"Yeah, for sure," I agreed. "I'm Aimee. What's your name?"

"Allison!" she hollered before running off toward the younger cabin.

That night, over a dinner of spaghetti in the "mess hall," we learned the rules of the camp. Every day we would be assigned a specific horse for the day, and it would be your job to find your mount (and in some cases, catch your horse if he or she was in a field), and groom and tack them up before your lesson. Each horse and his or her tack would be inspected by your counselor and given a grade of green, yellow, or red before you were allowed to mount. Failure to curry, brush or tack up correctly resulted in demerits. Three demerits and you were sent home. And I did not want to go home.

Some girls had brought their own horses to camp, but for most of us, it would be a smorgasbord of ponies and horses throughout the 14-day period, culminating in a two-day show attended by our parents before they scooped us up to go home. Outside of daily lessons and other horseback adventures such as trail rides, vaulting lessons and horsemanship, braiding and grooming courses, we would have time for swimming, "foot jumping" and hanging out. At night, after finishing dinner in the dining hall, campers were shuffled over to the bleachers of the facility's main arena where we cleaned bridles while watching the stable's private clients take jumper lessons under the arena lights.

By day three or four of camp, I was settling in and having a blast. Just that morning, I'd piloted a 13-hand stockily built pony nicknamed "Mad Mountain the Killer" around the outdoor cross-country course, sailing over "liverpool" water jumps and through the trees. The day before that, I'd spent the morning trying out dressage on a dappled grey named "Jiminy Cricket," followed by an afternoon jumping with bareback pads "on the wire" -- instead of a bridle, you steered your pony around the course via a steel wire looped around their neck.

And the night before, in our room, which featured three sets of bunk beds housing six girls with one shared bathroom, I'd giggled late into the night with a few of my new roommates, including two sisters with the last name Anka (Amanda and Alexis, daughters of Paul) and another with the last name "Holbrook" (yep, related to Hal) and another named Paula Firestone (of the Firestone fortune and sister to a later "Bachelor" from the hit ABC show). The next day, we were all supposed to try vaulting for the first time, which is essentially gymnastics performed on the back of a moving horse.

Sometime in the wee hours of the predawn morning, however, I began to feel a deep and dull ache through my abdomen and lower back. What the heck? I thought. Did I eat something bad? Where is this stomach ache coming from? When I woke a couple hours later to find bloody underwear and a stained bottom sheet, I realized the problem.

For the first time in nearly seven months since my first period ever, Aunt Flo had decided to pay me a visit again. While to an adult, the arrival of one's period can be a slightly messy inconvenience, to an adolescent girl who is the youngest of her peers to hit puberty, it can seem like a devastating crisis of epic proportions, the world's most shameful and humiliating occurrence. I honestly didn't know what to do. Not only did I lack any sanitary product of any kind, but I was also far, far too embarrassed to ask for help from anyone — not even our assigned barrack counselor. And the idea of asking any of the other girls if they had a pad (tampons were a foreign concept in those days for me), was absolutely unthinkable. I'd rather run through the campgrounds naked than admit, God forbid, I had gotten my period.

Panicked, I decided to feign sickness. That morning, complaining of a fever and stomachache, I begged off of riding or leaving the room, while all the other girls scampered off to the stables. When everyone had cleared out (and after devising a temporary solution using rolled up toilet paper in my underwear), I found a way to the phone and called my mom.

"Honey, you're being ridiculous. I'm sure one of the other girls will have something for you to use. You need to tell someone, at least your counselor," my mom said, trying desperately to reason with me.

"I can't do that!! You don't understand!! This is so embarrassing!! No one will ever think the same of me!!" I wailed.

In the end, my mom must have reached out to the camp management, who spoke with my counselor on my behalf, who — much to my deepest embarrassment — found a way to get me a box of pads and talked me into leaving the room and getting back in the saddle.

Toward the end of the two weeks, we were approaching the end-of-camp horse show and many of the girls were lounging about in the shade of a tree watching each other take turns vaulting on the back of a stout chestnut circling the instructor on a lead line.

"Hey Allison, is that your dad?" one of the counselors asked, and we all looked up.

"Hi girls," said the tall greyish blond-haired man with a slightly familiar drawl as he approached the group of young girls. We looked up at the towering, lanky figure. He certainly seemed much, much older than my dad or the dads of most of my friends. But a couple of the counselors across the way were whispering. I heard one say, "That's Clint Eastwood — oh my god …"

Wait, THE Clint Eastwood, the movie star? Wasn't he that guy in that movie with the orangutan?

"Hello, I'm Aimee," I said, looking Alison's dad in his slate grey eyes that feathered at the corners and offering my hand as the other girls and counselors gathered around. "Hello, there, little lady!" he responded in a gravelly yet friendly voice.

Clint, like all the parents, had arrived for the end of camp show the next day.

JUNIOR HIGH AND BARN BOYS

When September rolled around, it was time to head back to school for seventh grade at Los Cerros Junior High. Still painfully self-conscious and taller than all my peers, I had at least found a small posse of girlfriends with whom to navigate the tricky adolescent social scene. One of the most charismatic characters in my life during this period and throughout high school was my fellow horse-obsessed friend, Nicole.

A year earlier, on the first day of sixth grade, a lanky olive-skinned girl with dark brown eyes and wavy dark locks had walked right up to me in homeroom to introduce herself. "Hi. I'm Nicole Cohen, of Irish Sand?" she said, referring to the show name of her horse, against whom I had competed with my pony, Cindy, a few years back.

Ridiculously tall and striking even as a pre-teen, Nicole towered over everyone in the school - boys included. By the time we graduated high school, she stood 6-foot-one in stocking feet. And her personality was often as outsized as her physical presence. To say I was thrilled to find another bona fide horse girl at school who was also taller than all the boys (and me) was an understatement.

Like our house, Nicole's home also featured a small barn and adjoining pasture where she kept a bratty Shetland pony named Tuffy and her aforementioned horse, Sandy. She had grown up doing 4H and Pony Club and later trained with several different riding instructors around the Bay Area. Shortly after we met, she began trailering her horse to Farfetched Farm for weekly lessons.

It wasn't just horses Nicole and I bonded over. Honestly, by 13, boys had started to compete fiercely with horses for our attention and mindshare. After school, even while mucking stalls at her house or between lessons at the Jones' place, we frequently whispered and giggled about our current crushes, which boys and girls "liked" who, and gossiped about who was making out with who at the Golden Skate that weekend.

"Oh my god! Did you see Dave McIntosh and Ashley Walker going behind the lockers after couples skate?" I whispered as we walked our horses back up the hill after a lesson. "I can't believe she likes him!"

"No way," Nicole agreed. "He's gross. I thought she liked Eric McAfee anyway. By the way, what are you going to wear to the Christmas Dance?"

While most of our nonstop adolescent romance chatter remained among ourselves, sometimes we shared some of our musings with an unlikely listener -- Greg, a 16-year-old boy who worked for the Jones' as a barn hand for Farfetched Farm. Cheerful and friendly with twinkling, mischievous green eyes and an infectious grin, Greg was more than happy for the companionship of Nicole and me while he was in the stalls, tossing manure into a wheelbarrow. Draping ourselves over the top of the stall doors while he worked, we'd share every minute detail from conversations we'd had at school, notes passed and other trivial interactions we'd had with our current crush. "What do you, think, Greg?" we would ask, honestly hoping for his "older guy" wisdom on the mysteries of teenage boy behavior.

As you can imagine, over time, this somewhat one-sided "friendship" with Greg evolved into a full-blown teenage girl crush. Unlike the scrawny, immature boys in seventh grade, Greg was "cool" and totally "got" me. He liked great music like "Led Zeppelin" and "Blue Oyster Cult," and enjoyed talking about TV shows like "Cheers," tipping us off to what was popular among the football player crowd at the local high school we would soon be attending. In my mind, Greg must secretly be in love with me, and if I was just older, he would certainly want me for his girlfriend. In the meantime, we could simply be "best friends" and I could pretend to my friends at school that I had an older beau they didn't know about. That way I didn't have to worry about feeling like a loser who nobody wanted to ask to dances or go steady.

THE MAXI TAXI

While boys had started to crowd into my middle school mind space, horses still had the upper hand, and I was riding as much as ever. With Velvet gone, it was time again to get creative, and this time the answer came from Mrs. Jones. Red, one of the horses she had been given to care for, was available for "sponsor" — essentially a month-to-month rent situation enabling me to ride and compete at the higher 3'3" level required for the 12-14 age division.

Red, whose show name was "The Maxi Taxi," was a thickly built and rangy deep chestnut quarter horse who had been ridden by a few other Farfetched Farm Fillies over the years, often to championships. Standing a stout 16.1 hands and featuring a white diamond on his face, Red was a talented hunter with a classically athletic jump style — i.e., arched lowered neck and well tucked, even knees over every fence. Even-keeled, steady, reliable, and honest, he lacked any of the unpredictability of most of the mares I'd ridden in the past. And at nearly 20 years old, Red had seen and done it all — he knew his job and held few surprises for a decently skilled rider, as I had become by that point. I was lucky to get him for a mate and I knew it.

Red at Santa Barbara

Thinking back, a steady if the slightest bit boring, gelding was probably exactly the right fit for an emotional and increasingly hormonal teenage girl like me at that time. I did love riding Red, and he steadfastly and earnestly piloted me around the handiest of hunter and equitation rounds for the next two years, even as the fences continued to rise. We racked up championships at some of the bigger shows such as the annual summer Golden State show in Santa Rosa and even Santa Barbara, where he helped me throw down a round in the Onondarka Finals that earned me a place in the ribbons (eighth) above girls riding mounts worth tens of thousands of dollars more.

Red and I at the Santa Rosa summer show

However, while I loved riding Red, I wasn't "in love" with him. Unlike the earlier days of pure joy and borderline obsession I had felt for Quest and Cindy, both of whom I dreamed about at night, worried about all day, and would have willingly slept at night in their stalls if it was allowed, Red was a steadfast companion and a suitable mate. I knew I was lucky to have him. But he didn't truly hold my heart in the same way either of my mares had. Honestly, it might have been the first instance of what I later called the "perfect on paper" syndrome that plagued dating life through my 20s, when I would date young men with all the right credentials (good college, good job, good looking) who just didn't make my heart pound or bring out the butterflies in my stomach.

At the same time, I was riding consistently but feeling increasingly emotionally distanced from my mount, I had entered the social minefield of high school. While middle school had its challenges, this new era filled with the added pressures of older boys, cheerleading tryouts and kegger parties, along with a turbulent home life with divorced parents and my mom's new live-in boyfriend, was a whole new level of crazy.

Some time in my eighth-grade year, my mom had hooked up with a new boyfriend about seven years her junior in a classic rebound relationship post-divorce. Within months of dating, he had moved into the Diablo house crowding our space with his loud, obnoxious laugh and late-night binge drinking. I generally avoided him as much as possible, preferring the company of my friends or my boyfriend Jimmy over being at home in his presence.

So, in a story as old as time, my interest in riding and competing in shows eventually began to wane. For the first time, I didn't have my eye on the next prize. In fact, I was fairly confident that I didn't have what it took in terms of a horse or my own abilities to jump to the next junior age division (15-17), which required jumping 3'6" courses.

On top of all that, money was really tight. Following the divorce, my father had moved to Los Angeles to pursue a new career in entertainment. As a single parent, my mom was working full-time and struggling to pay the mortgage on the Diablo house, even renting out a room to a series of young women to help offset the bills. There was little if any cash left over to finance shows, let alone a new horse.

By the start of my sophomore year, I'd officially ended the sponsorship on Red and stowed my Farfetched Farm tack trunk and saddle into the rafters above the garage. Riding was my childhood, and it was time to grow up now.

Unfortunately, the boyfriend interpreted this "temporary break from riding" as a permanent retirement. One day I returned home on a Saturday afternoon after a sleepover at a friend's house to find him supervising a garage sale at our house.

"Hey," I said as I walked up, wondering what he and my mom had pilfered from the attic to make a few bucks.

"Hey," he repeated back. "I have about forty dollars for you — from your saddle and trunk."

So, to put this into perspective, he'd sold my irreplaceable blue and green with the Farfetched Farm logo custom tack trunk worth hundreds of dollars even in 1984, as well as a solid leather, perfect condition Crosby Prix de Nation saddle - also worth hundreds of dollars and of priceless sentimental value — to some random Joe down the street for less half the price of a Sony Walkman. Needless to say, this stupid, careless act put that boyfriend my "enemies for life" list faster than any of the other abuses he'd already committed against my brother and I by that point.

"What the hell! NO!" I screamed, staring at his disgusting face, shocked. "How could you? I never put those things out to be sold! I might start riding again. Oh my god! Mom??"

But no matter how much I shouted and pouted, kicked and threw things against the garage door in protest, the trunk and saddle were long gone and there was nothing anyone could do to bring them back. Perhaps, I started to think, it really was some sort of a sign that I needed to truly move on from horses and start thinking about the next phase of life — school, boyfriends, eventually college. My two heart horses – Cindy and Quest – were both long gone now, and most of the Farfetched Farm Fillies were graduating and planning to move away to college. It started to seem that horses were simply a precious part of girlhood that was fast fading into the rearview mirror now inched toward adulthood. After all, there were parties to attend, SATs to study for, friend drama to navigate. Where did horses fit into all of that?

The next day, I asked my mom if I could move out of my childhood room overlooking the barn with the tiny deck smelling of honeysuckle into the larger bedroom down the hall. Part of the move to the bigger more "adult room" involved boxing up the show ribbons lining the walls, shelving my horse show trophies, and even putting the framed oil painting of Quest into storage in the garage. The horse girl was growing up.

PART III:

ONCE A HORSE GIRL

REDISCOVERY

I've come to believe horses are just somehow in my blood, an obsession that spikes and fades intermittently through my life but never leaves me altogether. Which is why it shouldn't really have been a surprise that early spring day a few months into my 30th year when yearning for horses seemed to spring up out of nowhere during a hike to the beach in Marin County. My boyfriend and I were happily crunching through the gravel of a trail through Sausalito's Tennessee Valley. Looking up to the left of the trail, I noticed a rustic horse stable nestled into the state park lands and a few horses trotting around an arena.

"Wow, I never knew there were horses over here," I said. "How cool. I wonder if they have lessons?"

"You should check it out. That would be fun for you," Nate encouraged me. As an avid surfer whose own outdoor hobby occupied most of his non-working hours, he was eager for me to rediscover a passion of my own.

Within a week, I'd signed up for weekly lessons at the barn. Far from a show barn, this was a very casual beginner program with about a dozen rusty school horses and no jumping. And after 15 years out of the saddle, going back to the basics sounded perfect to me. It was amazing how much I had forgotten — from how to pick hooves or put on a bridle to posting the trot or asking for the canter. Unlike the old saying, it wasn't really "just like riding a bicycle." I did have to relearn just about everything, and it felt good to be doing that in a low-pressure environment surrounded by first-time riders and kids.

However, within a few months of these rudimentary walk-trot-canter flat Saturday afternoon lessons and a few breathtaking trail rides through the Marin headlands on the stable's assortment of quarter horses and Arabs, I was starting to feel ready to step it up a bit. Knowing it was doubtful, I could afford to ride at the level of my youth again, I still longed to jump again. I remembered that one of the assistant trainers who had worked for Brooke Jones' trainer, Mousie, was now based in my hometown operating her own stable there, and I decided to pay her a visit.

BOUNDARY GATE

Rounding the corner from the suburban sprawl of Eastern Danville and the Blackhawk outskirts, suddenly the landscape opened up into wide open expanses of golden grassy knolls dotted with black grazing cattle. On the right-hand side, framed by a fringe of tall Eucalyptus trees was a green and yellow painted sign reading "Boundary Gate — English Riding lessons, Hunter-Jumper training." Pulling into the gravel driveway adjacent to a covered arena, I slowed to avoid two cattle dogs that ran out barking alongside the car. The dust arose in a plume around my car as I pulled into an empty spot between the ranch style house on the property and the first of two barns.

I could hear Heidi's voice shouting out commands to riders in the back arena before I even shut the car door and headed out back.

"That's right. Left leg, let him go. Don't hang on to his face! Good ride!"

A dark bay with a tall woman rider galloped by as I neared the back arena. Seeing me, Heidi waved and walked toward me. Slight but sturdy in stature, she was not the same strawberry blonde, freckle-faced 19-year-old I remembered from my youth. Instead, this was an intimidating and accomplished equestrian who commanded the respect of both her horses and riders. I felt both nervous and excited.

"Hi," I shouted. "Heidi, I don't know if you remember me, but I used to ride with Lowrey Jones at Farfetched Farm. We used to show with Mousie when you were her assistant. My name's Aimee Grove. I heard you were training out here and I wanted to check it out," I explained.

"Hi Aimee. Sure, I remember you," she said, striding closer in her dusty boots and breeches.

"I just started riding again after 15 years away. I was wondering if you had room for another student?" I asked.

"Sure. I have a few horses I can put you on. Why don't you come out on Saturday morning around 10."

And so it began again. This was the first of two returns to riding as an adult for me. I took another 13-year break a few years later when I started a job in San Francisco, got married and had a baby. But again, I returned to riding when a career change provided a more flexible schedule and that familiar equestrian itch returned.

After finding a new barn and trainer who offered a fleet of lease horses, I picked right up where the teenage Aimee left off. Suddenly shopping for new clothes, hitting the gym or even going out with friends took a backseat to grabbing saddle time whenever or however I could get it. Eventually,

I bit the bullet and committed to a half-lease on a slightly cantankerous gelding named Magnus, an arrangement that guaranteed three lessons a week on the same horse.

Magnus was a pretty cool guy. Boasting a long stride, easy lead changes, a fairly decent motor and adjustable pace around the courses, he had many positive attributes. But Magnus was also sour and sullen on the flat, rarely motivated to move forward unless pointed toward a fence. Attempts to get him moving off the leg were too often met with dead halts and hi-ho-Silver rearing.

My heart yearned for a beloved horse of my own again, something I truly loved and cherished, adored riding alone and in lessons and shows. I dreamt about it every night, after spending hours researching horse sale websites and Facebook pages and doing calculations in my head about how to afford the astronomical costs of horse ownership (let alone the price tag of the horse itself). I started a secret "horse fund" in my business savings account where I socked away every extra dollar I could realistically justify according to my modest (by equestrian world standards) income.

AND THEN CAME LUC

It isn't often as an adult we get the chance to experience overwhelming, exhilarating -- heart-bursting -- infatuation. You know, the kind of euphoric excitement of receiving your first puppy or kitten, or the earliest days of a brand new, first romantic love relationship when it feels like you literally can't stop thinking, dreaming and talking about the object of your obsession.

But that's exactly how I find myself today as the proud "new mom" (i.e., owner) of a magical unicorn named "Luc." After four years of dreaming and searching, scrimping and saving, trying one "not quite right" mount after another, many tears and much anxiety and discouragement, I've finally found "the one." And thank God, I didn't settle because he's 100% perfect for me in every way.

Luc arrived in early spring on a van from Canada. I'd been told he was Bay, "cute," 13-years old and very snuggly -- a key trait since my prior trial horse had been a biting, kicking hormonal mare with a nasty stop that dethroned me more than three times in a month … exactly opposite of snuggly.

At first glance, he looked attractive, if a bit shopworn from the winter clipped coat and rubbed out mane from the long trailer ride to California. A big-boned, thickly muscled and round 16.2, Luc sports four white stockings and a striking white blaze down his face -- what we used to call "flashy" back in the old days but now is more popularly described as "having lots of chrome."

But after years of riding and trying so many different horses, one thing I've learned is that being pretty is fairly low on the priority list in being an ideal companion and mount for me. Sweet and affectionate demeanor, kind eyes and calm enough to rest his head in your arms for a hug? These are the true magical qualities ... and Luc has them in spades. His previous owner described him as "More Lab than horse" and she's right. Luc defines the "in your pocket" personality type described in so many horse ads. One day I came to the barn on a Sunday afternoon and caught Luc lounging in the shavings taking a snooze. Even when I came into his stall to join in, petting his head and neck, he decided to hang out for a bit more rather than scramble to his feet like most horses do in that situation.

In addition to being a sweetheart on the ground, Luc is a dream under saddle. Like a good-natured, amiable dude, he simply does his job, trotting along with pricked ears, dropping his head to collect when I get my legs adequately wrapped around his barrel and picking up a softly loping canter with a slight tap of my outside heel. Want to slow down? A "whoa" and sinking into my heels does the trick. Jumping Luc is similarly stress-free. He has a motor but listens when I settle back, eagerly takes me to and over any fence I point him to

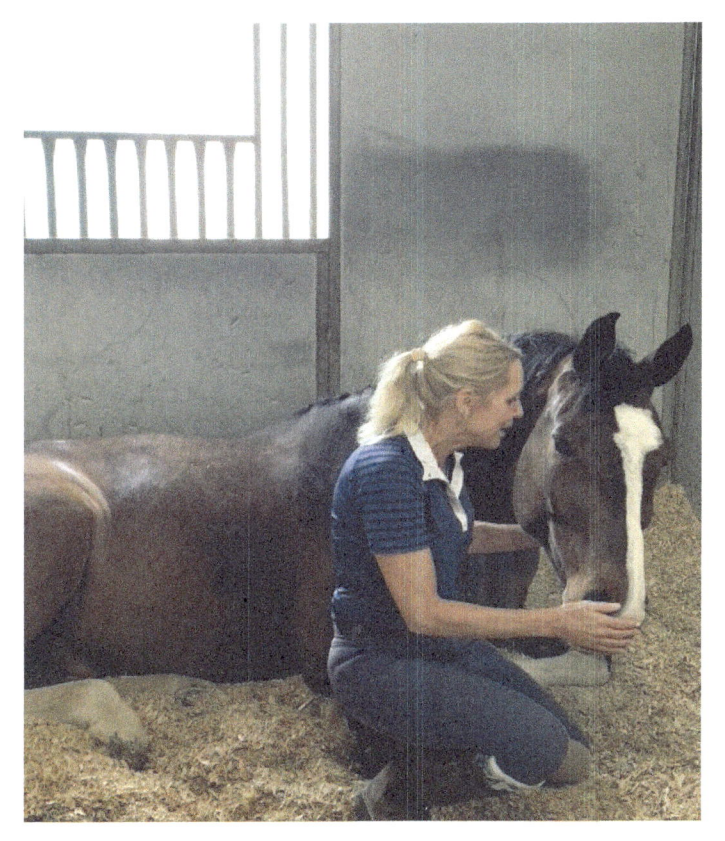

"Luc" taking a Sunday siesta

even when I goof up judging the distance or do some other stupid thing. He's smooth and comfy approaching and crossing the fences and -- this is key -- never scares me. Oh and yes, he's ridiculously, stinking cute too!

Am I obsessed? A thousand percent yes. After a lesson, I am sad hopping off his back, and leaving the barn for the night makes me sad. Yes, there are times I just want to hang out in his stall to watch him nibble hay and breathe in his air … I literally just want to be around him.

As weird as this infatuation may be, it also feels both familiar and right to me. When you've found your heart horse, you just know. I had this with Quest 40 years ago and Luc's giving me a second chance at that kind of life-changing love. I can't wait for our future adventures together.

Finding Luc and settling in with my new barn friends who share this passion – fellow horse-crazy girls, men and women, ranging in age from 12 to 70+ – is a bit like finding my way back to Farfetched Farm. He's my heart, and this is my home.

My "heart horse" Luc

❖ ❖ ❖

Made in the USA
Las Vegas, NV
28 July 2023